Greekling

Greekling

Kostya Tsolakis

Nine
Arches
Press

Greekling
Kostya Tsolakis

ISBN: 978-1-913437-82-4
eISBN: 978-1-913437-83-1

First published October 2023 by:

Nine Arches Press
Unit 14, Sir Frank Whittle Business Centre,
Great Central Way, Rugby.
CV21 3XH
United Kingdom

www.ninearchespress.com

Printed in the United Kingdom on recycled paper by Imprint Digital.

Nine Arches Press is supported using public funding by Arts Council England.

Supported using public funding by
**ARTS COUNCIL
ENGLAND**

Στους γονείς μου,
Ακριβό και Βασιλική Τσολάκη,
με αγάπη.

Contents

Greekling

noun

a small, insignificant, or contemptible Greek

... *και μέτραγα κουκί κουκί τα αισθήματα,*
τίποτα δεν αγάπησα, κανένας δεν μ' αγάπησε.

– Ανδρέας Αγγελάκης, «Έπειτα ακόμα»

Fantastic failures of journeys occupied me...
– Charles Dickens, Great Expectations

The party was always somewhere else, at someone else's place.
– Derek Jarman, Modern Nature

Kifisos

sad river of Athens
    no one loves you
        no Tiber or Seine
    no one sings   *Κηφισέ*
Κηφισέ τι όμορφος
    που είσαι upriver
      an unspoiled pocket
    lucid waters   planes
in leaf sieve the sun
    an ephebos   his mother
      by his side   sacrificed
    his childhood locks
long like eels   sleeked
    with olive oil   to your divine
      current   millennia later
    barking dogs chained
to your banks warn
    of what expects you
      downstream   your sacred
    groves and sanctuaries
replaced by factories
    pharma labs   industrial parks
      refuse sullies your body
    forms a lurid rainbow
skin   tossed rubble blocks
    your flow   culverts
      and concrete canals
   confine   reroute
your natural course   boxed under
    a jammed motorway
      no good comes out of you
    fish you were home to

barbel   Marathon minnow   chub
            gone   no monument marks
                        your drab mouth   cleaved
            by a crumbling jetty
you meet the bay to noise
            a looping interchange
                        the anchor drops
            from millionaires' yachts
chirping sparrows swoop
            down   peck your greasy face
                        as if in thirsty farewell
            in summer you turn
into a stagnant thing
            dry up   stink   the city
                        remembers you exist
            only when it pours
tenses as you swell   become
            a sweeping   turbid torrent
                        threatening to overflow
            overwhelm   Athens wishes
                        you did not exist

Another Shore

Language is never taught but eaten
in its fruit: σύκο, πεπόνι, καρπούζι, βερίκοκο.

    Quarrels are hard-to-snap sea urchins
full of the roe of making up. How can you stay mad

    at the man asleep in the tamarisk's shade,
cicadas needling the hot afternoon, a wasp's thimbleful

    of pain coasting his body, skin draped in the salt
        of the morning swim.

The Case of Vangelis Yakoumakis

In this marshy ditch, overlooked by naked branches,
lies the decomposing body of Vangelis. He studied

at the dairy academy nearby. Missing for thirty-seven days,
he was sighted all over Greece at once. The press

described him as *sensitive, a loner*. Bullies slapped him
while he ate. When he showered, they turned the water off.

Someone kicked him down a flight of stairs, someone
locked him in a closet, made him sing for hours. Then

the video: six sniggering guys piling on top of him. Thousands
heard Vangelis beg, *Please stop, you're hurting me*, his voice

smaller than an olive. All this was recorded. So was the knife
found at his side. What's lost are his features, the smooth flesh

on his cheek, where his mother would kiss him
                                        goodbye.

Tribute of Children

Many of the conscripted boys achieved fame and fortune, rising as high as grand vizier, and sometimes parents volunteered their sons for the devshirme. But these arguments do not soften the harsh reality that for many if not most Greek families, in which ties of kinship have always been particularly strong, the removal of a son was a heartbreaking loss. – David Brewer, *Greece, the Hidden Centuries*

The men came, lifted us
like marble from the quarry.
A dozen budding boys –
graceful, well-bodied. I was
the youngest, no taller
than her waist, clinging
to her thigh like wax-drip
on the candlestick. Did she consider
hiding me – down the rope-cut lip
of the well, behind the thick-
threaded kilim, half-finished
on the loom? (I recall an eagle
snatching a hare; a blood-red sky.)
Did crushing my good hand
in the olive press cross
her mind? Slicing my cheek
from eyelid to jaw? But they saw me
before she saw them. As they marched us
out in our changeling uniforms –
crimson caps and tunics
paid for by our families – she watched,
stone silent, while the other mothers
shrieked and wept. I turned,
smiled for her, as if to say: *I will
return.* Hoped she'd hold on
to my promise like the bone

fragment of a miracle saint.
And here I am. A grown man,
my beard longer than my hair was then,
fostered by another mother
tongue, but still her son. Back
to kiss her hands. In the vine-choked
courtyard, I announce myself,
but the name I answer to now
gets no response. Yanked from deep
inside me, my former name – the one
she gave me – is cold, gritty
in my mouth, like coffee dregs
with no future to tell. *That boy
is dead*, her voice darts – dark,
stinging, a path at night overrun
by nettles – through the gap
in the door. *I just stepped out
a minute*, I laugh, begin
to tell her how I plan to lift
our village, build baths, a covered
bazaar, a humpback bridge, so no one
risks wading the frothing, muscled
waters of our river. I tell her how
at court I wear a white kaftan
lined with lynx, my turban
has a golden band, my voice
sets hunting dogs off, returns
falcons to my calfskin arm.
I list my titles, triumphs, ties
with such important people
but the more I talk, the more

my words are dry, a honeyless
hive. My brothers – gaunt, tawny,
callused versions of me – say
since that morning, all she does
is spindle, darn their socks, scrub
and scrub the hearth. That her sleep
is restless, as if the quilt she lies
under is stitched with glass
and rooftile shards, that she only
leaves the house for Sunday liturgy,
to venerate my grave. *Go away*, stings
her voice again. *Whatever your name –*
you're one of them.

Ghazal: Of Them

Long summers home from uni, we still pretend: I'm not one of *them*.
Those men on the news at eight. The all-gay cruise. Mum makes fun of them.

She reads things, hears things, is told things. The ills it latches onto
the body, mind. One's standing. Stare-into-nothing agony spun of them.

All I can think of: in England – not checking myself. What I say, how I look.
The handsome lads in the clubs. How I love. Every mother's son of them.

Why did you buzz your hair? That shirt's too tight. Constant opinions.
I miss the eager rays of eyes my body catches. The sun of them.

Home is Trash Palace, The Joiners, Ghetto. Dance floors where boys
unfurl, bloom. If I was king, I'd have portrait miniatures done of them.

You won't ever let anyone harm you? Mum lets loose from behind
the battlements of the morning papers. That loaded gun of them.

In the close sticky hold of the darkroom, a name is null. Men go by
touch, taste, smell. All the different selves I put on? I'm none of them.

My childhood bed – host to just one body. I fall asleep counting kisses:
at parties, in toilet stalls, other beds. Head spins – the sum of them!

At the airport, Mum lets go of her Kosti. I, Kostya, hold fast, know
who I stand among: those men, my found kinfolk. Glad to be one of them.

1981

Men sit in smoke-filled cinemas, screen-
lit eyes fixed on Harry Hamlin's Perseus –
his tight-muscled frat physique, dimpled chin,
conditioned chestnut mane. Fired up, they seek

a taste of this demigod – his life-giving nectar –
in those other cinemas that constellate
the city's seedy roundabout. Fellow mortal men
is what they get. The broadsheets they carry

for some semblance of propriety, cushion
their knees, protect neatly ironed trousers
from the grimy carpet, sticky velour seats.
Buried in the columns: the first recorded cases.

Naming It

The cause of the disorder is unknown. Researchers call it A.I.D., for acquired immunodeficiency disease, or GRID, for gay-related immunodeficiency. – The New York Times, 11 May 1982

We sweat all night, soak
our beds, fill wards, spill
out of hospitals, slurry
the roads. We die
under dripping awnings,
in tavern yards, in barns.
Experts name it after us,
kids add it to the things
you catch in tag. They say God
brought it down, it came
in a foreign ship, you catch it
shaking hands, sharing cups.
People in high places get it,
holy men, teachers, national treasures
after a hundred deaths on stage.
Those who haven't rush past us, bolt
their doors, seal their heavy windows.
Leaders tell us they are *on it*,
that doctors spend all day
and night looking for a cure,
but really they are busy with diplomacy,
with how the nation looks abroad.
All the while, our shrouded corpses
carpet the steps of government,
and we run out of paper
to list our dead.

1991

Myths-obsessed, I watch it over and over
on tape – unfazed by the mishmash of tales,
the liberties taken. Too young to fault its cheesy
dialogue, the jerky stop-motion monsters, I lap it up:

the catchy, triumphant score, the gods' soft-
focus palace, the fumbling clockwork owl. I root
for Perseus, naturally. My body can't articulate
yet the pull of this all-round hero, his semi-divine

anatomy. I spare no thought for his nameless
companions, their unheroic deaths. Stung
by giant mutant scorpions, petrified by virulent
Medusa's flashing gaze – who cries for them?

The Light-up Snowman on the Balcony

Cheap plastic thing. Through smear-free
glass, your gentle glow allows the boy

to survey his room – this ordered universe –
as he falls asleep. The cared-for spines

of illustrated books: Greek myths, great
civilisations, the illustrious lives of explorers

and conquerors. The silver-plated protector-
saints above the headboard. On the white-top desk,

stapler, hole-punch, magnifying glass,
laid out neatly side by side. Every colour

in the pencil holder, sharpened to a point. Spikes
that wall a fortress. The slatted wardrobe

doors, behind which everything – t-shirts, pyjamas,
underwear, socks – is ironed to perfection.

You clutch a candy cane – striped red and white
like a barber's pole or barrier tape – look smart,

the boy thinks, in your black top hat, green
scarf wrapped snuggly round your neck.

Your affable smile reminds him
of that flying snowman in the film. The boy

has his pilot dad for that. Dad who sees
to the tree: from picking it with the care

of an emperor choosing his heir, to hand-
sawing it apart, on the Feast of the Lights,

to be fed, branch by frayed branch,
to the fireplace. And the smell of burnt spruce

lingers for days. Mum will pack away the decorations,
carefully wrap the gilded baubles she's had

since childhood. She expects the boy to pass them
down to his own kids – those vague-shaped

creatures, still viable in his mind. Each year he asks
for you, Snowman, to be kept out: *All year, yes.*

It's a queer request. *Imagine,* Mum laughs,
the light-up snowman on the balcony

– in July! What will the neighbours think?
Such unorthodox desire.

Phimosis

On this front, they join forces, as if the line
relied on it. Music channel on, I lie back
on a towel on their bed, turn my face away
to the sketched female nudes above the headboard.
My parents follow, to the letter, the doctor's instructions[1].

It burns, stings. A rubber band stretched to its limit.
Bearing it without a peep earns me *Good boy* after
Good boy. I think of when my auntie caught me
prising the rosebuds open in her garden. *Μπουμπούκι,*
she said, *you can't force them before they're ready.*

---

1. *Over time, the muzzling should ease. For now,*
cleanse him once a week. Gentle retraction,
a little at a time, is OK. With a lukewarm compress
of camomile, wash the exposed head, wipe away
any collection of cells. Pat dry. Return to normal.

Bathroom in an Athens Suburb

All I have are guidebooks
from archaeological museums –
page after page of glossy athletes,
gods and heroes in bronze
or marble, some missing limbs,
noses, heads, others full-bodied.
At first, I'm happy to look, flick
through their fractured perfections.
Growing bolder, I will them off
their pedestals, let them stretch
after millennia of posing, grant them
a heart, pulse, sinew, permeable
skin. They let me examine their scars
dug by ploughs and anchors. I close
my eyes, inhale the earth that clings
to tangled hair, the iodine sweat
of those raised from shipwrecks, ignore
the ochre scent of Mum's cosmetics
on the wicker shelf. Locked behind
this door, I don't want to come out
but as summer nears,
it gets harder and harder
to breathe.

freedom or death

Fire and axe to those who submit!
– Theodoros Kolokotronis, Greek general, one of the
leaders of the 1821-29 Greek War of Independence

on garlanded days
we wear the flag
our scratchy blue trousers
or skirts   starched
white shirts stiff
as the principal's call
to attention   a boy
short back and sides
pure-gloved   brandishes

nine syllables   sky and sea
into assembly   flanked
by two girls   bobs
lacquered to perfection
reverence hardens
our olive expressions
we sing of heroes
whose feats   we're told
granted us freedom   men

whose laureled names
live on as stadiums
avenues   ferries
gilt-framed   they border
our teenage vision
how unfettered
they look compared to us
flamboyant silk turbans
bright red fezzes

tight-fitting jackets
embroidered with gold
flowers   griffins   mermaids
and other unnatural
creatures   waxed moustaches
point east and west
their waves of hair belong
on angels   their eyes
are sparked fireships

betrayed
by their own   impaled
drowned in sacks
garrotted   skinned alive
their heirs sold off
renamed   recultured
on shuttered nights
when my mind feels free
to submit to bodies made

like mine   they seek me
in bed   ungloved
carry me to a narrow
coastal pass   unspool
my desire   tie
my brittle wrists
with it   *redseed*
they hiss   their yatagans
unsheathed

On First Reading Cavafy's 'Caesarion'

Final period Greek. My fingers sore
after a day of tight-grip biro scribblings, I jot
the date and poet's name on the handout.

We've been kept on a refined diet
of Elytis and Seferis. This namesake
of mine is new to me. I offer to read aloud.

Over the first ten lines, my tongue negotiates
a language both familiar and a touch
archaic, standoffish, as the poet mocks the self-
proclaimed grandness of an ancient dynasty
hell-bent, like my own family,
on keeping up appearances.

But then, turning the music on
in his voice, the poet's fantasy summons a lad
a year older than me. A final son of his line,
rubbed out by spiteful men, as he blocked
their path to history. A featureless shadow
(I note NEGLECTED in the margin)
re-fleshed by feeling, compassion.

The poet lets his lamp go out. (HE LOVES
THE DARK.) His own Caesarion shows up
at the threshold: near-dead, an almost-
man, his beauty oddly enhanced
by the tired sadness of a boy who's lost
his place, his mother, his voice.

I run my tongue over my teeth – seeds
stuck in my braces from the fuzzy-skinned fruit
I bit into. Tangy, sweet. The burst of pinkish juice
spills from my mouth, down my chin, stains
my shirt, the gouged white plastic of my desk,
the sheet through which desire has finally spoken.

My classmates, one eye on the clock, carry on
yawning, doodling, writing down the lesson.

No one notices the mess I've made.

Prickly Pear

My spiny pads sprout from one another: punk-
purple buds grow from my flesh, become
hardened pith. A queer transfiguration. Unlike
others of my kind, I was never a mortal changed
by a god's terrible love. But my yellow yellow
flower sits beautifully on young men's sun-
burned ears. And there are lanky boys who wish
to be like me. In the stuffy gloom of childhood
bedrooms, narrow frames they've long outgrown,
August sizzling outside, they wish for something
tougher than their mother's thorny bougainvillea –
for spikes to wreathe their nipples, for my green
scales, to feel the eagle's talons digging deeply
enough to lift them from their teenage sleep.

Days of Summer, 1998

Being sixteen grants me entry-level rights to the city.
Pocket money for my taxi rides, a toastie, water, juice.
Conditions apply: back by 8pm; a payphone call home
every two hours. My suburban cosmos (wet clover,
peeled eucalyptus bark) ends just past the grey concrete
O of the open-air mall. That retail Coliseum never took
off; Mum's video rental shop, lower ground floor,
ruined in the flood of '92.

The rear-view mirror reflects an acne-flushed teenager.
I wear Dad's gold-rimmed aviators, hope they make me
look, if not cool, a little older. Through petrol-tinted
lenses, I skim the advertising boards that crown family
businesses lining Vouliagmenis Avenue: mattress
wholesalers, 4X4 dealers, parquet layers, joiners,
security door and window installers. All that makes
a home. I read until I feel queasy. A huge red apple,
2D flesh unbitten ever since I remember, dominates a
junction. Waiting for green, the taxi driver whistles,
Look at that skirt, asks me, *Have you fucked yet? I bet it's
all you think about.*

Let out in the hubbub of Syntagma Square, I'm
conscious of the steel rodent stitching new lines
under my feet. On the other side of metal panel walls
plastered with posters for Attica Metro and Athens
2004, the ancient skeletons of boys that never made it
past my age are being collected, piece by brittle piece,
into plastic zipper bags. Bones stuck in the throat of
the city's slow progress.

Slicked by the nagging drip of air con units, pavements are a craggy, mottled terrain: shattered marble slabs, pebbledash tiles, worn-out cuts of Karystos slate. Wounds patched with cement. Everything I walk on grates.

Zigzagging up the tan limestone bulk of Lycabettus, I think of my teacher who said the hill's name could mean *where wolves prowl*, or – in a language no one speaks anymore – *shaped like a woman's breast*.

At the summit, the effort of the climb plucks a score on my hamstrings only my body can hear. I wish for this endless surrogacy to end, for Athens to deliver adult me, in full armour, into England's outstretched arms. Below, the city's reassembled altar smokes diesel and meat-grilling fumes from a thousand souvlaki joints. On the rooftops, solar panels sparkle like flecks of quartz in sand. My desire could peel this city.

Traipsing back down, the dog's breath heat boils my head like a hoplite's tight-fitting helmet, bronze dimpled by repeated battles.

At the café terraces of Kolonaki, overhead fans blend the dense, closet-like air with the nutty aroma of premium cigars, the loud musk of overpriced scents spritzed a-few-too-many times on yoga-taut necks. Monogrammed businessmen squabble over shares, commodities, mergers – grownup stuff – sit elbow to elbow with pearled grande dames, veteran hacks with ice cream scoops for ears, society minglers in head-to-toe white. Empty designer wallets nurse a watered-down frappé for hours.

Mum drilled into me: *No one's better than you.* I ought to claim my spot in this wannabe Rome, sip iced tea, watch the blasé members of this gilded tribe. But the brusque, pleated waiters may judge my t-shirt the wrong shade of green, my centre parting not centred enough, order me to stand before my backside has even landed on a front-row chair, chase me off with a rolled-up copy of *Kathimerini.* Humiliation that'd still burn on my deathbed.

I find shade in Dexamenis Square, under a young plane tree, on the bench by the statue of Elytis. The great poet – straight-backed, one foot, kouros-like, forward – gazes firmly ahead, into whatever dead poets gaze into. The mid-afternoon glare keeps the playground empty. No time for children to be out.

Tonight, the open-air cinema screens *City of Angels.* In one scene, a man lies dying in hospital. Seth, a dewy-eyed angel in a long black coat has come to escort the man's soul to heaven. Angels are meant to be unseen, unheard by humans, but the man – an ex-angel, mortal since his fall – senses Seth. A vestige from his former angelhood. I wish I could sense my own kind too, tell them apart in a crowd. Breastbone glowing pink through their skin, perhaps.

A plank of a man – forty or so, thick salt-and-pepper beard – joins me on the bench, tweed flat cap at odds with the heat, his short-sleeved linen shirt, ghost of a white vest showing under custard yellow. A pale ring of skin where his wedding band should be. He offers me a Lucky Strike, slightly bent, from a crumpled packet. *No, thanks,* I say, afraid that even touching it will make me smell of him.

Lighting up, the heavy smoke he puffs fraught with
frustration, he grumbles something about a lawyer,
about queues, forms, fees. Clocking my age unleashes
a string of platitudes – unasked-for bits of life advice
I've been given many times before by men who see in
me an ephebos to be inducted in their ways. I forget
it all, apart from this: *Leave*, he says, standing up,
crushing his fag underfoot, *this country gobbles up its*
children.

chatroom '99

```
***you are in m4m_europe***
caesarion81 enters
```
                    dial-up debut
                            unschooled desire
                                    seeking his tribe
```
@caesarion81 stats??
```
                    multicolour cascade
                            acronyms emoticons
                                    babel of shorthand
```
@caesarion81 hung top iso nsa
```
                    cyberslang confounds
                            rigid
                                    precise english
```
@caesarion81 i <3 a twink
```
                    look listen & learn
                            never prepared
                                    for this exchange
```
@caesarion81 in2??
```
                    errant education
                            disconnect from
                                    ivied expectations
```
@caesarion81 lol i mean what u rly in2 ;)
```
                    breathless adolescence
                            gives way to
                                    fostering alterity
```
@caesarion81 u like poppers?
```
                    a virtual window
                            a way out
                                    a way in
```
caesarion81 exits
```

First Time

I wear the white Versace shirt,
one size too big, Mum bought me.

We meet in Thissio, sit outside a bar
with a view of the Temple of Hephaestus.

He looks different from the pic he sent –
balder, heavier. But he has a smooth voice,
the kind they use in milk or yoghurt adverts.
I lie about my age.

I have a Moscow Mule in a coral bottle.
He drinks something in a heavy-bottomed glass.
We talk about our summer plans.

A taxi takes us to a place north of Omonia Square.
In the dark hotel reception, he pays
5,000 drachmas. A blue note. I don't contribute.

Even with the window open, the room stifles.
On a tray, laid out like wedding rings,
two condoms.
He keeps the light off.

I'd expected lovemaking to be
a soft, easy affair –
a seaside room,
the scent of lemons,
lapping waves.

Instead, this angular, stinky wrestle,
and his voice turning childish,
he calls me *baby*
as we soak the bedlinen.

We dress in the dark.
We don't kiss goodnight.
If there is blood on the sheet,
it isn't the sort tradition expects
presented from a balcony.

ode to Ari's blue shirt

as worn by Alex Dimitriades in *Head On* (Australia, 1998, dir. Ana Kokkinos)

We wanted to be part of our Greek culture and we needed to rebel against it.
– Ana Kokkinos

o synthetic threads   shade-shifting
        poly-satin Aegean blues
                stretched by this other restless Greek

body   his dislocated queerness
        a reflection of mine   o fuck-me shirt
                o hit-the-tiles armour   brown-eyed

like me   his accent is a world away
        but the coiled-spring lad
                soaking your fabric is a soldier saint

broken free of a Byzantine icon
        o garish stitch   in this   my buffer year
                not out to anyone   but in England

at last   you rouse me like a nation's flag
        spur me to cut loose   spear through
                eighteen obedient years

o all-night garb   *put me on*
        you pronounce   *forget your tight little world*
                let the hungry hands of men undo me

Full Retraction

What does it in the end
is wet mouth after wet

mouth of men who can't
speak my tongue. *Careful,*

I instruct until
I no longer need to.

London Fields

we fucked through spring and summer / I'd cycle to you after work / you'd greet me at the door in just a towel / I think your name was Rich / your room was always in a mess / your bed was up against the open window / I loved the silky fuzz that ringed your navel / we'd cum then lie down for a bit / two lads naked on our stomachs / the breeze would cool the sweat off us / we'd peek out through the half-raised blinds / the couples clinging on the grass / the red-faced barbecuing dads / felt sad for them all wearing clothes

on the dance floor at Heaven

after Sappho

he seems to me from another planet
    that lad who   pint in hand
glides up to you   stands close
    drinks in your alcopop voice

& tonic laughter   boy it
makes my heart flit in its cage
    just one look at you & no sound
can exit my throat

    my tongue crashes   low
fire grazes under my skin
    eyes   useless   thumping
bass burrows in my ears

    & I'm drenched   trembling
all over   a dull glow stick
    how I seem   to me
        is good as dead

marble bf

But a Greek would never think of a charioteer like this.
– Historian Dr Michael Scott on the Motya Charioteer

hip cocked out sassily   muscular body
a long   sensual S   hand pressed
ever so lightly into
uncannily soft flesh
no hero's nakedness
for you   sleeveless   rippled-sand
chiton clings
with the sweat   the effort
of the race you won
sheer fabric teases   suggests
you're hung   your cock
unlike the reserved slugs
of other   sober ancients
whose toned   no-nonsense
nudity embodies
the manly ideals of the polis
your snail-shell curls
are archaic   but I've seen
your pouting lips
on stern-browed models
in Italian fashion spreads   I've seen
your puffed-out chest strapped
in a leather harness   as you dance
in a Vauxhall club   dilated
eyes looking at no one
and everyone at once
the fierce rocks
of your buttocks belong
to the ballet dancer I slept with
once   my disbelieving hands
exploring his range of muscle

one delicate dawn   marble lad
camp   sexy   mysterious
you can't be a charioteer
a rich man's lackey   maybe
you're the sun god   clocking
out after a long day's ride
on your blazing   risky chariot
or perhaps you are
some tyrant's trade   great
on the lyre   skilled at reciting
all the big Homeric hits   a rent boy
put in this get-up for a kink   sculpted
by the best Greek hand
money could buy   an extravagance
a folly   a sybaritic joke   I know
my ancestors   their eyes
would see offence in you
standing on a pedestal in the agora
in your cocksure go-go
dancer's pose   dressed
like a woman   well-endowed
I think of you often   I too
have stood on the margin
of what it means to be Greek
to be a man   have tasted dirt
because of it
I travelled far to find you
charioteer   on this salt speck
of an islet on the tip
of Sicily's tongue   this place
that isn't Greece

anymore   nowhere
near home   if you opened your mouth
what strange idiom
would come out   if you tried
to explain how you got here
I wouldn't understand   I open
my mouth   hobbled Greek
comes out   the vocab
of a gangly   closeted teen
the odd one out
among your peers   you survived
because you were trash
your bashed face   the pockmarks
on your torso   betray
your ending   dragged
through the city   dumped
as wall-fill
shameless beauty often ends
like this   unquarried
you were safe   lying deep
for millions of years
in the pale marble seam
no one yet had called *flawless*   I too
was safe when still unqueried
so awkwardly   by others
in your bed of sun-baked clay
you slept until
the bristled kiss
of the archaeologist's brush
woke you   in the spotlight

of this dusty museum   cracked
screens zoom in
#masterpiece #excellence
#bodyperfection
I recognise you
for the curious   unbelonging
thing you truly are
masc   femme   Hellenic
foreign   a Greekling
made like me

Nocturne for the American Boy
I Pulled at Popstarz

What was your name? I pick
through layer on igneous layer
of all my hook-ups, crushes, loves,
find no trace of it. Time
leaves behind only the hardiest material:
your nipple piercings,
my gold baptismal medallion.
Other details of our night together
just about retain their shape: holding
hands on the top deck of the night bus
transporting us to my dinky room
in Bayswater; your slender body, even paler
than mine; your hair – black, straight,
obscuring your forehead. But your face?
Beyond recollection. What's intact
is the thrill I felt watching
as you stripped for me –
your naked silhouette caught
in the blinds' silver lines, the false
dawn of the fire-escape lights.

Strange Pilgrims

*GHB and GBL can reduce people's inhibitions, and some people take
the drugs to have more intense sex. –* talktofrank.com

They prayed for incorruptible bodies,
for voices in their heads to stop
their sermons. Guided by the orange glow
of digital shells, they rode trains
to end-of-the-line places
they'd never have otherwise known.

Their hosts administered communion,
measuring drop by bitter drop, at bedsides,
kitchen islands, in sitting rooms with views
of motorways. Tingle-fingered ecstasy
came first: everyone blossomed, crowned
with blue chemical halos.

Lips left ex-votos of spittle all over
their skin, tiled lino floors slipped from under
their feet, limbs lifted as every insult
that clung like wax melted away.
Then came the test some call *going under*,
others *wrestling the devil*.

Senses suspended, they lay on sofas
or tangled flokati rugs, while the others watched.
Many minutes passed, sometimes an hour or two.
Those who came back reported no memory
but showed bruises and bleeding tears.
Those who failed shivered themselves off

in torrents of sweat, turned their eyes
to their brains and were gone.
They were mourned, of course they were,
but their prayers for total release had been
answered. Look for them online. Frozen
as young men, smiling forever, incorruptible.

Nobody

My host, whose threshold I crossed
half an hour ago, who offered me a drink
in a plastic tumbler, who asked me to talk him
through my tattoos, is turning me onto
my stomach. Kissing my back, he whispers
his plea. Again I laugh it off. *Please,*
his voice is saying – but his body's telling me
the time to negotiate is over. I discover
what it's like to be a flower pressed
under a dozen volumes on a drawn-out
civil war. He spit-hooks himself inside me.
Lightning bolts up my spine, splits me.
And each half will seek the other forever.
I'm left with the smell of sweat
and poppers gone flat on his pillow,
a muddied running shoe in the corner. I'm split
into before and after photos. Twenty-eight days
of hard-to-swallow pills, in case he spilled
a new kind of life into me.
No compassionate god will come,
turn me into something small and winged
to slip away.

Kostya as a Failed State, 2011-13

A found poem using excerpts from news articles and analysis pieces on the
Greek financial crisis, published in the international press in the early 2010s.

1.

Downgraded to junk status.
How did it even come to this?
What did Kostya do wrong?

2.

The upheaval is undermining the traditional family structure,
pushing Kostya to leave his homeland for better prospects.

Kostya must have misunderstood something:
the point of a liberation is not to knock yourself out.

It wasn't a good time, said Kostya,
grumpily clearing the plates from table six.

3.

Kostya's parlous state
has been widely blamed on years of mismanagement.

Successive Kostyas have studiously ignored
the principle of discipline
and even doctored data to conceal their mischief.

The ordeal shows that living up to lofty idealism
is never easy.
An ideal that Kostya imagined for himself.

It is the shock of undercut expectations.

4.

A walkout brought the crisis to a head.
The depth of the problem was revealed:
G___ offered solutions that, rather than fix the problems,
simply let them fester.
G___ warned that he was looking at Kostya with a view to
possible downgrade.
If G___ and Kostya break up, Kostya will not be able to
survive, with all the consequences that one can imagine.

The Kostya issue:
BEWARE OF KOSTYA BEARING BONDS.
If you can't fix Kostya's problems, at least quarantine them.

Kostya would have been equally screwed if he stuck with G___.
Kostya's dependence on G___ would only have increased.
Kostya's rescue-or-not saga could drag on.
Kostya's woes reflect badly on the credibility of G___.
An already volatile equation.

G___ regretted that Kostya had reached this point
but it was best to clear up the uncertainty,
decide whether they want to commit.
Yes or no?

5.

Kostya stalled for time,
disclosed his deepest feeling.

There was shock and surprise on their faces.
They were not sure how to grab hold of the issue.

Kostya begs
(a monumental mess,
never stood a chance)
facing ruin
and still begging.

What is so remarkable about this episode
is that it was not so remarkable at all.

6.

As the dust settled, it emerged that Kostya
was teetering on the brink of depression.

7.

The crisis has exposed
the central weakness,
fault lines.
Sometimes Kostya ignores facts. He runs on psychology.
There's no good way out of this.

8.

Kostya's crisis is a crisis of identity
as much as anything else: indolent sloth,
cheat and liar, master of corruption.
The fraudster in the family.

Kostya has been the butt of jokes.
The implication is always the same:
Kostya is lazy and doesn't like to work.

Still on shaky ground,
Kostya faces a confidence vote.
Unless Kostya redefines himself –
a radical overhaul –
this could become the perfect catastrophe.

9.

The hardship is as much psychological as economic.
If Kostya were a company, he would be bankrupt.

A bankrupt has to turn everything he has into money.
Sell your islands, you broke Kostya
... and the Acropolis as well!

It is clear that belts must be tightened.
The lights could soon go out.

10.

Sinking deeper into the gravest crisis,
Kostya is no nearer to finding an exit from his woes.
Kostya's meltdown could negatively impact,
a 'Kostya contagion' could spread.

Neighbours are on edge. A worried world is looking on.
A toxic mix of anxiety and fear hangs in the air.

11.

Hotlines have been set up offering rewards
for people who inform on Kostya.

US President Barack Obama called
for greater efforts by Kostya to contain his crisis.

There is even a boom in sales of tarpaulins
to cover Kostya and make him invisible
to aerial inspectors.

European leaders are meeting to attempt to resolve Kostya's crisis
and prevent it infecting.

Minister, do you still have confidence in Kostya?

Yes.
I always try to put myself in someone else's shoes. Kostya has to live with
enormous resistance, in his own heart.
When Kostya struggles to such an extent, he deserves our respect.
Those who cannot master these challenges on their own must be helped.

12.

For Kostya, the future is a void,
and anger and helplessness dig deep in Kostya's psyche.
Frustration at his predicament continues to boil over.

Coping with a looming catastrophe,
hard-bitten, hard-pressed,
Kostya wrestles with a groaning and glacial depression.
And if nothing changes?

Anastylosis

noun: the restoration of a ruined monument or building by reassembling fallen parts and, when necessary, incorporating new materials.

...the ammunition store ignited in a vast explosion, [...] blowing out the centre of the building, smashing 28 columns, parts of the frieze and the internal rooms that had served for church and mosque.
– Mary Beard, *The Parthenon*

Have you any idea what it's like to blow up after two millennia of holding it together, feel your roof rip open, your sides unstitch? That flaming mortar shot! And to think I was holy. Processions of tongues – agalma, iconostasis, mihrab – prayed in me. Unhallowed, my very best marbles were up for grabs – lording tourists helping themselves to slices of frieze as if at a buffet. The garrison recycled my less attractive fragments, turned triglyphs, simas, geisa into lintels, cisterns, windowsills. Spolia on family homes.

Riddled with bullet holes. My joints scavenged for lead. Overnight I became a symbol, charged with restoring a nation's sense of self. Everything judged foreign was scraped off this history-crowded hilltop: towers, battlements, houses; the boxy mosque that sprang from my gutted core. First attempts to reassemble me, raise my felled drums, the ashlar walls of my naos, were rough-handed, misplaced. If it fits, it fits. Rusting iron clamps swelled up, cracked already broken parts. Now I'm fed titanium. Skilled craftsfolk take me apart, record, place every piece of me back where it belongs, care for it like it's newborn, not just a battered bit of stone. Stonemasons patch my wounds with quarry-fresh material, cut to perfectly match what's lost, shattered or nipped by pollution – take pride in recreating, not imitating, the work of their predecessors. Untarnished white, evidence of trauma, will with time turn honey-brown, impossible to tell from the rest of my patinaed body. Shown off to visiting monarchs, presidents, celebs, I'm a must-see, an item on a bucket list, admired because there's nothing straight about me, built to trick the eye. See how the entasis in my columns, the gentle inclination on my stylobate and architrave, lend me faultless proportions and balance? Endless flows of visitors, kept in check by the trill of whistle-happy guards – *No shirtless! This is Sacred Rock! No touch!* – congregate around me, led by guides who exalt me as the pinnacle of a golden age. Faultline city, horizon-breaching megalopolis – in our entwined lives, what have I not suffered for you? Admit it, Athens. You'd be nothing without me.

Sparrow

The day before the royal wedding,
rainbow flags jostled for air
with Union Jack bunting. Neon flyers –
pumped lads in aussieBum briefs – hawked
weekend-long parties at the clubs. Pacing
Old Compton Street, I rang my dad.

I could have sent Yiayia to tell them. At breakfast,
perhaps. Pink dressing gown
over her nightie, carried up two floors
by her fluffy slippers – the angel
with the message. If it came out
of her mouth like a velvet ribbon, surely
they couldn't turn their faces from it? Mum
looking at her scrambled eggs
as if they were vomit.

On the other end of the line, Dad said: *It's all right*,
in the careful voice he used
when talking to sparrows –
those curious little things,
so easy to frighten, that perched,
hollow-boned, on the railing
as he tended his delicate balcony plants.

I, Wonky Nose

Tilting slightly to the left, still plagued
by spots and blackheads. Where haven't I led you?
Those basements in Berlin, where the heavy brew
of damp and piss made my nostrils flare; the bleach-
scoured corridors in saunas – the air thick
with the unsorry, almondy smell of wired men
fucking. And what is London but my recollection
of every stranger's shower gel you lathered with –
iced mint and lemon, peppercorn oil, geranium leaf –
after a no-strings meet in Kilburn, Battersea, Bow?
And remember New York? Its most lasting souvenir
is Manhattan's humid July breath, laced
with the fungal stench of trash, palm-greased
bucks, the wheaty sweat of go-go boys dancing
in tatty jockstraps at The Cock. I admit, harsh light
doesn't favour me. It's true, my ridge
is not a seamless extension of the forehead.
I'm not the kind an ancestor would feel inspired
to sculpt. But wasn't it a lover who called me
wonky, kissed me tenderly on my hump?
Have I not sniffed a lad's freckled shoulders,
like a faithful terrier, made him laugh?
And how about those giddy nights buried
in salt-sweet armpits – didn't I sing?

Patrick

It surprised me,
your body responding to mine
like birdsong.

All those years ago.
It was summer,
and you were alive.

A flint blade,
your drunk tongue,
it skinned me.
I only knew your first name.

I only knew your first name;
it skinned me.
Your drunk tongue,
a flint blade.

And you were alive:
it was summer
all those years ago.

Like birdsong,
your body responded to mine.
It surprised me,
Patrick.

what a shame,

this precious galaxy of spit
shooting out of my mouth

onto the gum-infested kerb
this sober Sunday morning

not into the coral throat
of a kneeling lad on boots-

only night at the Vault –
his wide-open eyes, fixed

on the driblet hanging off
my lip, saying: *you & I*
                    are earth

The Dead of the Greek Enclosure in West Norwood Cemetery Speak to Me

For our exclusive set, only the best:
pink granite, Portland stone, architects.

Our tongues were glossed tiles
fired in Eton and Harrow. Orthodox names,
tough meat for English mouths, recast
as *Bobby, Alec, Jack.*

In death, our accent is emphatically Hellenic:
competent bodies, turned redundant bones, housed
in solemn Doric temples, barrel-vaulted mausolea,
fine marble sarcophagi carved
with sphinxes, laurel crowns, alphas and omegas.

Wheat ears and bolls of Egyptian cotton
festoon our memorials. Clues
to all that made us rich, chewed away,
irreverently, by black mould and pollution.

Mutton-chopped gods of commerce,
spunky shipowners, benefactors,
cornerstone-laying fathers
of a close-knit diaspora rest among us.

Beloved wives of the above.

We never truly called this island *home.*
Its soft-edged climate. Peephole sun.
Egos we bested on hardwood trading floors
called us *intruders, wily Easterners,*
a downgrade from our famed forefathers,

more turned on by a deal in wool
than a lecture by Socrates.
Even you, visitor,
our homeland buried in your teeth,
find us alien, struggle
with our epitaphs' ossified Greek
that pulls its hair in grief, offers tearful libations.
You frown at our pairings:
uncles matched with nieces, cousins
with cousins. A handful of dynasties trading
their teenage sons and daughters.
Trust, kinship, hierarchy, cohesion
made waterproof through marriage bonds.

Your peculiar hunger
does not quite fit our criteria, your body
has no currency among us.

Why are you here this cawing afternoon?
Why stumble on this rumpled, sodden ground
that lilts our mossy crosses, threatens
to uncap our graves? So what
if you find solace in your name –
a trip hazard outside our enclave –
repeating on slab after slab? So what
if you think us mislaid
in this grey suburb, opulent monuments
looking forlorn, vandalised doors
boarded up, vaults sloppily patched
with unadorned concrete? So what
if no one lights a candle for us anymore,

leaves no offerings
but crushed beer cans
and mildewed cigarette packs?
We and our memorials are here to stay.

Will you ever call this island *home*?
For now, you're breathful, uncased.

When they scatter you against some wind
or other, who'll remember you?

Go back to your mother. Your xenitia
has been a kind of death to her.

Vine

Gift from my forefather,
green calligrapher, tell me,
do your roots absorb
every voice cast
in this yard? Endless
Easter feasts, arguments,
the breaking of terrible
deaths. Each leaf you bear,
a word from an ancestor.
I pick them, fill them with
rice, mint, dill. My mouth
tastes sweetness. In tile-
searing heat, I sit
in your cool, watch
the black-and-white cat cling
to your fraying, twisting
bark like I cling
to our name – I,
your very last leaf
closest to the blank sun.

Someone Else's Child

It was a lynching. There's no other way to describe it.
– A witness to the killing of Zak Kostopoulos
in Athens on 21 September 2018

I undress, watched over by medals for bravery
and life achievement awards in Dad's study, sleep
on mismatched sheets in the new sofa bed – stiff
mattress unyielding to my shape. Square-jawed,
great-uncle Grigoris – army coat too big
for him, battle-muddied boots – stares straight
out of his thumb-smudged picture frame.

Morning. The mountains that penned in
my childhood are covered in snow. Dad mutters
in the hallway: *The Archangel has abandoned me.*
He keeps silent over lunch, eyes fixed
on his soup, as though afraid he's close
to using up his allocated words. Walking to the café,
he hands me his cane, won't take my arm.

The bow-tied waiter shakes Dad's hand, calls me
by my dead half-brother's name. I don't
correct him, neither does Dad. Untouched,
his espresso grows cold. Now and then a spinning
light speeds by, washes his face a watery blue.
So much police, I say. He doesn't respond. I want
to tell him how, minutes from here, someone else's

child, made of the same material as me, was made
immaterial. How buffed boots, ordered to prevent
and quell, judged him a bone-snatching stray, infected
with god-knows. How they pinned him, handcuffed,
against the rough, uneven pavement, kicked his heart
in. A Friday lunchtime in this city. But your weary
expression, Father, clamps the words to my throat.

Korai

The Acropolis Museum, Athens

Spring sunlight blunts   the clean masculine edge
of the stark museum hall   the polished marble floor, stocky
concrete pillars. Years ago   my eyes paid these girls here
little attention, drawn as I was   to their gym-fit brothers.
To the herded, rushing tourist   the girls may seem like clones:
formal, column-like stances   shoulders back, heads
held up straight. An archaic   deportment class. Insipid
plaster replicas gather dust   in public service waiting rooms.
They're employed to smile   out of sunbleached *Live Your Myth
in Greece* posters tacked   on ferry ticket office walls. But spend
some time with them and   you'll see, no two korai are the same.
This one holds out a dove   another offers a pomegranate.
Some wear a heavy, blousy   peplos, others are more lightly
dressed in pleated chitons   or wrapped in the cloak-like himation.
This kore has curves. Another   uniquely, puts her right foot
forward. The soil that hid them   sucked out the expensive paint
they were coloured with: ochre   malachite, hematite, Egyptian
blue. So, it's hard to discern   the bands of rosettes, rhombuses,
the birdlings on their clothes   that made them stand out
from each other. Their famous   smiles, too – meant to show
they stood above the hardships   of this world – range from genial
and gods-blessed to something   coaxed out for a business shot.
You begin to notice fractures   the places where these daughters
of Athens were welded back   together: wrist, neck, elbow. Even
the less-than-fragile waist   You notice lobbed off noses,
hacked-at breasts, buttocks   malleted scalps. Try to picture
the cyclone of axe-wielding   hands that struck the citadel –
that extra furious energy it took   to torch, tear down, cut up
these limestone girls. The stunned   Athenians who returned,
gathered the sullied fragments   buried their damaged, tongueless
daughters in a pit. Right there   where it happened.

Tamarisk

Sailing time from the capital: eleven hours. Part
of what ferry operators call *the barren line*. Mum
says on the phone, *They used to exile people there.*

For Tim and me, it's our craggy, crowdless paradise.
Most mornings, we have the dirt path to the beach
to ourselves. Sometimes, there's a leisurely gay couple,

also seeking paradise, we need to overtake. I wish
to have my portrait painted against this backdrop
of dry stone-walled hills, copper-gold at sundown,

overspread with peppy sage, the purple works
of thyme, deep-green caper shrubs – long stamens
launching from its showy white flower like violet flares.

I like this tree, Tim says settling in its dense scale-leaf
shade after his dive. *Αρμυρίκι*, I say. I don't know
the English for it. We learn not to ask what bolted

winter is like here, this place where the school is next
to the cemetery – generations of islanders crammed
in whitewashed ossuaries. Not to mention

the pirate raids that shipped every soul away to trade.
That a blackened, desiccated mast is all that remains
of the agave's single flowering. I find that *αρμυρίκι*

is *tamarisk*. Deep-rooted, it fringes coastlines, thrives
in saline soil, grey-brown bark nourished by sea spray.
Is, I suspect, the tree carved on the immaculate, white

marble stele that commemorates the hundreds exiled
to the island. Back then, ships would anchor offshore,
new arrivals brought to land in dinghies. Now, things

are straightforward: tourists charge off a stern ramp,
fresh claimants of our haven eyed by us already
here. How many people can you fit in paradise?

On Rereading Cavafy During Lockdown

There you are, namesake, tracer
of half-remembered pleasure.

I read your words until darkness
covers them, see your shadow
in the corner: a hunched figure,
unguarded eyes behind round spectacles.

I too have put down words that defy
those who wish to retouch my desire. I too
write from outside the bounds of Greekness;
yet how Greek we are in doing so.

Each time I read your words,
you offer my lips, with a steady hand,
a tall, cold glass of water –
to wash the fruit down.

Notes and Acknowledgments

The definition of 'Greekling' is from the Merriam-Webster online dictionary.

'Another Shore': The title of the poem is taken from a line in Constantine P. Cavafy's 1894 poem 'The City' (Greek: «Η Πόλις»).

'The Case of Vangelis Yakoumakis': In 2019, a court in Ioannina, north-western Greece, where Vangelis Yakoumakis was a student at the Dairy Vocational School, found eight of his fellow students guilty over their role in causing Yakoumakis to take his own life in 2015 after months of bullying. The guilty verdict was upheld in 2021.

'1981': What would later be named acquired immunodeficiency syndrome (AIDS) was first reported in the 5 June 1981 edition of the *Morbidity and Mortality Weekly Report* (*MMWR*), the epidemiological digest for the US published by the Centers for Disease Control and Prevention (CDC).

'freedom or death': The title of this poem is the English translation of Eleftheria i thanatos (Greek: Ελευθερία ή θάνατος), the motto of the Hellenic Republic.

'ode to Ari's blue shirt': The Ana Kokkinos quote is from *'Head On': The film that helped change Australian culture* (Con Stamocostas, Neos Kosmos, 14 January 2019).

'on the dance floor at Heaven': This is an 'after' translation of Sappho 31, also known as 'φαίνεταί μοι', a lyric poem written in Aeolic Greek by Sappho of Lesbos (c. 630-c. 570 BC).

'marble bf': Unearthed by archaeologists in 1979, the Motya Charioteer is on display at the G. Whitaker Museum on Mozia, a small island off the western coast of Sicily. The quote is from the 2013 BBC Two programme 'Who Were the Greeks?', presented by Dr Michael Scott, Professor of Classics and Ancient History at the University of Warwick. 'marble bf' is dedicated with friendship and admiration to Seán Hewitt.

'Anastylosis': The passage from Mary Beard's *The Parthenon* (Profile Books, 2010) refers to the 1687 siege of the Acropolis, during which the Parthenon, used by the defending Ottoman garisson as a shelter and to store gunpowder, was hit by a Venetian mortar. The passage in full: 'In the end, the inevitable happened and the ammunition store ignited in a vast explosion, killing as many as 300 people (usually forgotten in the story of archaeological tragedy) and blowing out the centre of the building, smashing 28 columns, parts of the frieze and the internal rooms that had served for church and mosque.'

'Someone Else's Child': On 21 September 2018, 33-year-old LGBTQ+ campaigner, HIV activist and drag performer Zak Kostopoulos, also known as Zackie Oh, was brutally beaten up by two men after he entered a jewellery shop in central Athens seeking protection from street abuse. In video footage, four police officers are seen to be violently arresting Kostopoulos, while one officer is seen kicking him. According to the forensic report, Kostopoulos died from the multiple injuries he sustained. In May 2022, the two men that initiated Kostopoulos' beating were found guilty of participating in his killing. The police officers, also accused of contributing to Kostopoulos's death, were allowed to walk free. The poem's epigraph is from *'Zak's an icon': the long fight for justice over death of Greek LGBT activist* (Helena Smith, *The Guardian*, 20 December 2020).

'Naming It' was included in the 2019 New River Press anthology *WHEN THEY START TO LOVE YOU AS A MACHINE YOU SHOULD RUN*.

'The Light-up Snowman on the Balcony' was commissioned by Candlestick Press and included in *Christmas Stories: Twelve Poems to Tell and Share*, published in 2022.

'London Fields' was first published in *Too Young, Too Loud, Too Different: Poems from Malika's Poetry Kitchen* (Corsair, 2021).

'marble bf' was featured on the website of *Poetry Wales* in August 2022, part of the 'How I wrote' series of interviews conducted by Zoë Brigley.

Thanks

My heartfelt thanks to the editors of the following publications in which poems from *Greekling* were first published: *Ambit, Anthropocene, Butcher's Dog, fourteen poems, Fruit Journal, Magma, Pamenar Press, Poetry London, Stand, Stone of Madness Press, The North, The Poetry Review, The Scores, The Tangerine, Wasafiri* and *whynow*.

'Bathroom in an Athens Suburb', 'First Time', 'Naming It', 'Nobody', 'Someone Else's Child' and 'The Case of Vangelis Yakoumakis' formed part of *Ephebos*, my 2020 **ignition**press pamphlet. My gratitude to Claire Cox, Niall Munro and Les Robinson for helping bring *Ephebos* to life – and a special shout out to Niall who kept the **ignition**press mailouts going during the tough lockdown months of 2020-21.

Thank you to everyone in my poetry 'village' for your friendship and support over the years: Romalyn Ante, Dean Atta, Stuart Bartholomew, Matthew Beavers, Mary Jean Chan, Theodoros Chiotis, Iulia David, Jim English, Katie Griffiths, Stephen Guy-Bray, Seán Hewitt, Alice Hiller, Uli Lenart, Jim MacSweeney, Mícheál McCann, Andrew McMillan, Konstantinos Menelaou, Jo Morris Dixon, André Naffis-Sahely, Astra Papachristodoulou, Rachel Persad, Peter Scalpello, Paul Stephenson and Piero Toto. Thank you, also, to my fellow members of Malika's Poetry Kitchen and to my good friends at the Poetry Translation Centre.

To Jane Commane – thank you for offering *Greekling* a wonderful Nine Arches Press home.

To Katianna Micha – I'm forever grateful to you for introducing me to Cavafy. *Greekling,* and my journey in poetry, began that late September afternoon in class in 1997 when we read 'Caesarion'.

To Heidi Williamson, my mentor and friend – thank you for guiding and cheering me on, over countless cuppas online and pints at the Green Dragon all these years.

To Tim, as ever, with all my love.